MADE
COMPLETELY
NEW

A STUDY IN THE BOOKS OF COLOSSIANS AND PHILEMON

BIBLE STUDIES TO IMPACT THE LIVES OF ORDINARY PEOPLE

Christian Focus Publications

The Word Worldwide

Written by Dorothy Russell

PREFACE

GEARED FOR GROWTH

Where there's LIFE there's GROWTH:
Where there's GROWTH there's LIFE.

WHY GROW a study group?

Because as we study the Bible and share together we can

- learn to combat loneliness, depression, staleness, frustration, and other problems
- get to understand and love each other
- become responsive to the Holy Spirit's dealing and obedient to God's Word

and that's GROWTH.

How do you GROW a study group?

- Just start by asking a friend to join you and then aim at expanding your group.
- Study the set portions daily (they are brief and easy: no catches).
- Meet once a week to discuss what you find.
- Befriend others, both Christians and non Christians, and work away together

see how it GROWS!

WHEN you GROW ...

This will happen at school, at home, at work, at play, in your youth group, your student fellowship, women's meetings, mid-week meetings, churches and communities,

you'll be REACHING THROUGH TEACHING

INTRODUCTORY STUDY

What can we discover about Colossae?
Look at the little map and find Ephesus, Laodicea, Colossae and Jerusalem.

At the time Paul wrote this letter Colossae was in the country known as Phrygia, now part of Turkey. Paul travelled twice through Phrygia, but it does not mention a visit to Colossae – see Colossians 2:1. How then had a church come into being there? Look up these references:

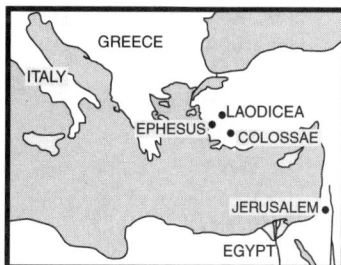

Acts 2:10	Who were in Jerusalem on the Day of Pentecost?
Colossians 1:7 and	
4:12, 13	Where does Epaphras fit in?
Acts 19:1-10	What happened when Paul was at Ephesus?

We don't know exactly how the church started or who God used. The important thing is that there was a vital church fellowship there.

Why was Paul writing to the Church?

The word 'heresy' in the dictionary is described as 'An opinion adopted for one's self in opposition to the usual belief'. Such a state of affairs can become the seedbed for the fermentation of religious sects and teaching which is either slightly off-centre from biblical truth or grossly unscriptural and even non-Christian. The following references will help us discover a little about 'sects'.

Acts 5:17; 24:5	What two 'sects' are mentioned?
Acts 24:5, 14	How is Paul described?
2 Peter 2:1	How destructive are the heresies mentioned?
Colossians 2:8	What heresy was creeping into the Colossian Church?
Colossians 2:18, 19	Discuss the error here.
Colossians 2:16-21	What were the traditional Jews insisting on?

Can you see how the teaching was coming through that faith in Christ alone was not sufficient for salvation.

How does Paul tackle this problem?

He says: 'Christ is SUPREME. You don't need Christ plus tradition, men's ideas, etc.' (Col 2:15-23).

Look up these verses and see what a wonderful Saviour we have. He is:

The Eternal God and Creator	Hebrews 1:2,3
Equal with God	Philippians 2:6
The Son of God	Matthew 3:17
The Image of God and the First-born of all Creation	Colossians 1:15
The Lord of Glory	1 Corinthians 2:8
Container of all wisdom and knowledge	Colossians 2:3
King of Kings and Lord of Lords	Revelation 19:16
The true Light	Luke 1:78
The Truth	1 John 5:20
Head of the Church	Ephesians 1:22
Author of Salvation	Hebrews 5:9
The Way	Hebrews 10:19, 20
The Life	Colossians 3:4
Mediator	Hebrews 8:6
Our Sustainer	John 6:35, 48

Why does Paul exalt Christ?

You already know, don't you? In the face of these glorious descriptions (we could spend a week on each title of Christ!) all we can say is:

'We have CHRIST. What more can we want or need?'

Paul proves his point. Any 'extras' that man would add to the finished, eternal work of Christ on Calvary are ridiculously superfluous.

The words of one of our old hymns put it plainly:

My hope is built on nothing less
Than Jesus' blood and righteousness;
I dare not trust the sweetest frame
But wholly lean on Jesus' Name.
On Christ the solid Rock, I stand;
All other ground is sinking sand.

STUDY 1

A LESSON ON PRAYER

QUESTIONS

DAY 1 *Colossians 1:1, 2; Acts 16:1-3; 1 Corinthians 4:17.*
a) Who wrote this letter? To whom was it written?
b) Who was Timothy?

DAY 2 *Colossians 1:1,2; Romans 1:1-6.*
a) What does your dictionary say about 'apostle'?
b) What qualified Paul for apostleship?
c) Are we all supposed to be apostles?

DAY 3 *Colossians 1:3-8; Colossians 4:12; Philemon v. 23.*
a) Why did Paul thank God for the Colossian Christians?
b) Who was their minister and what do we know about him?

DAY 4 *Colossians 1:3,9-12; Ephesians 1:15-17.*
a) How often did Paul pray for these two churches?
b) List the things he prayed for the Colossians.

DAY 5 *Colossians 1:9-12; Romans 12:1, 2.*
a) Put verses 9-12 into your own words and use them as a prayer for someone you know.
b) How can we be filled with the 'knowledge' of God's will?

DAY 6 *Colossians 1:11-14; (see also Eph. 2:2-9).*
a) How does God equip us to be 'partakers of the inheritance of the saints' (v. 12 KJV)?
b) Would you care to share with the group how you became a Christian?

DAY 7 *Colossians 1:9-12.*
a) Which of these things would you like others to pray for you?
b) Has this study given you the desire for a more vital prayer life?

Memorise Colossians 1:13, 14.

DEVOTION

Paul, as a Pharisee, was a student and advocate of the Jewish law. After his encounter with Christ (Acts 9:1-6) he became a GOSPEL PHARISEE! He said He was 'set apart from birth' (Gal. 1:15). Paul was utterly convinced of God's calling and an all-out devotee to the gospel. God still 'calls out' special people for special purposes today, but the Scriptures make it clear that all Christians should be devoted to serving the Lord and communicating their faith by what they say and how they live.

PRAYER

We can learn some basic lessons from Paul's prayer. Note how:

1. He THANKS GOD for His goodness to His children. It is only through God that good comes to us. PRAISE should be the major ingredient of every prayer.
2. He PRAISES GOD for the evidence of His blessings in the lives of His children.
3. He SPECIFIES three qualities which the life of Christ produces in us:
a) *FAITH* which brings us salvation by accepting what Christ has done for us.
b) *HOPE* takes us beyond the things of time to eternal realities.
c) *LOVE* transcends all the pettiness of human reactions and enables us to live in harmony with others.

GOD'S WILL

Are you finding that the Bible is PRACTICAL? It is not theory. It is 'how to'! Paul's desire is that the Colossians won't just KNOW ABOUT Christ but that their knowledge will work out practically in their lives. A growing knowledge of God (v. 10) applied in daily living will produce SPIRITUAL GROWTH. Romans 12:1, 2 gives the key to knowing God's will. We have to give ourselves over WHOLLY to God, WALK in OBEDIENCE to what He reveals, exchange earthly VALUES for spiritual ones and God's priorities will come into clear focus. As long as we think we know better than God we can never come into a real working relationship with Him.

OUR INHERITANCE

Have you ever read the 'missing persons' column in a newspaper? Attempts are often made in this way to locate someone who has inherited a fortune and does not know it! Just think, that person may be living like a beggar and unaware of how rich he or she is! It is possible to be a Christian, to know you are saved

FROM sin, yet to be living in ignorance of the fact of how rich Christ has made you. Ignorance doesn't nullify what Jesus has done! The Israelites were BROUGHT OUT FROM the bondage of Egypt that they might be BROUGHT INTO the freedom and abundant provision of Canaan. We don't deserve and haven't earned what Jesus has obtained for us. It is all ours through the grace of God.

Get busy. Search the Scriptures. Discover ALL your inheritance. Christ has brought us:

FROM the power of darkness INTO the Kingdom of Light.
FROM the devil's power and death INTO eternal life in Christ.
FROM being children of disobedience INTO being children of obedience.
FROM slavery to Satan and sin INTO being JOINT-HEIRS with Christ.

STUDY 2

THE GREAT CREATOR IS MY SAVIOUR

QUESTIONS

DAY 1 *Colossians 1:13,14; Hebrews 9:26; 1 John 3:8; 1 Corinthians 15:54.*
a) What three things has God delivered us from?
b) Look up 1 Peter 2:9 and Ephesians 5:8. What has God brought us into?

DAY 2 *Colossians 1:15-17; Hebrews 1:3; John 1:18; John 14:9.*
a) How do we know what God is like?
b) Look up John 1:1, 2, 14. When did Jesus come into being?

DAY 3 *Colossians 1:15-17; John 1:3; Hebrews 1:3.*
a) Who created everything?
b) How does everything hold together?

DAY 4 *Colossians 1:18-20; Ephesians 1:22, 23.*
a) What is the church?
b) Who is its Head and Source?

DAY 5 *Colossians 1:20-22.*
a) Why did God need to make peace with us?
b) Discuss what verses 21 and 22 mean.

DAY 6 *Colossians 1:22.*
a) What was the purpose of Christ's death?
b) How does His death become effective for me personally (Acts 16:31; John 1:12)?

DAY 7 *Colossians 1:22-23; 1 John 5:10-13.*
a) Is there room for doubt once we have trusted Christ?
b) What glorious hope is set before those who stand firmly on God's promises?

Memorise Colossians 1:21-23.

NOTES

Dad and David had a wonderful time during the Spring evenings. They were busy carving out a little ship in anticipation of a summer holiday by the sea. What care and thought went into the creating of their 'Bird of the Sea'. You can imagine the great joy David had sailing his boat on those long, lovely summer days. But one morning he got side-tracked from sailing. He met up with some lads on the beach and joined in their games.

Too late, he remembered his little ship! There it was, bobbing its merry way out to the open sea, too far away for David to reach. It was a very disconsolate boy who went home to tell Dad the sad story.

Surprise! Surprise! A few days later David saw his boat for sale in a toy shop. In vain he tried to explain to the shopkeeper that it was his property and that he wanted it back. 'You'll have to buy it, if you want it, lad,' the shopkeeper said.

Crestfallen, David went back to Dad and told him the tale. What do you think Dad did? Yes, he produced the cash for David who ran off triumphantly and bought back his boat.

As he walked home with the little craft in his arms he was softly repeating over and over again ...

> 'First I made you. Then I bought you.
> So you are mine TWICE OVER.'

That's exactly what God has done for you and me. He created us. The devil claimed us. But God redeemed us back to Himself at tremendous cost: the sacrifice of Jesus.

CREATOR

Jesus is God. Jesus has always existed. He has no beginning and no ending. He created everything and everyone. He takes pre-eminence over angels and all heavenly powers. He is the first-born of every creature. As CREATOR He is a revelation of God to us. We are overwhelmed by God's power, majesty and holiness, but totally blind to His purposes of love. We cannot comprehend His vastness, His eternity, the mystery of the Godhead. God wants to bridge the sin-gulf between us and Himself. But He, as Creator cannot reach us. God the CREATOR is too big for us to grasp, to understand.

SAVIOUR

God has a plan. He will come to us as man. Jesus comes as God revealed in flesh. Now we begin to understand. God wants to identify with us. But there is still the sin question. Then God's fuller plan unfolds. He wants to die for our sins. So in Jesus, at Calvary, the price of our redemption is paid. The Great Creator becomes our Saviour. Jesus takes away our sin. He conquers Satan and death. He lives. He reigns. All things are under His feet. Not because He created them. But because of His death and triumphant resurrection and victory over all the powers of evil. Jesus is far above all. God is no longer far off. He dwells in the heart of every believer. God is love. Yes, we know Him through the Lord Jesus Christ.

'Down from His glory, ever living story
My God and Saviour came
And Jesus was His name.
Born in a manger, to His own a stranger,
A man of sorrows, tears and agony.

Oh, how I love Him.
How I adore Him.
My Breath, My Sunshine, my All in All.
The Great Creator, became my Saviour,
And all God's fulness, dwelleth in Him.'

STUDY 3

COSTLY PRAYER

QUESTIONS

DAY 1 *Colossians 1:24; 1 Corinthians 4:9-13; 1 Peter 2:20-22.*
a) Since Jesus suffered to bring salvation why did His servants have to suffer so much?
b) Are we exempt from suffering?

DAY 2 *Colossians 1:24-27; Acts 9:15, 16; 1 Corinthians 15:3, 4.*
a) What was Paul's task?
b) What was his message?

DAY 3 *Colossians 1:27-28.*
a) Read verse 27 in several translations and discuss what it means.
b) Cite Paul's twofold aim in preaching.

DAY 4 *Colossians 1:29; 2:1.*
a) Pick out the words here that indicate Paul's deep concern for the Colossians.
b) To what does Paul attribute his ability to be so involved for God?

DAY 5 *Colossians 2:2.*
a) Paul was most concerned for the .... of his converts.
b) What brings spiritual prosperity?
c) What binds Christian hearts together?

DAY 6 *Colossians 2:2, 3.*
a) Who is the source of ALL wisdom and knowledge (1 Cor. 1:23-30 will help)?
b) Are the treasures of wisdom and knowledge hidden FROM us or FOR us (1 Cor. 2:5-16)?

DAY 7 *Colossians 2:4, 5.*
a) How real was Paul's identification with the Colossian Christians?
b) In what way did they give him cause for rejoicing?

Memorise Colossians 2:2, 3.

Paul's Task

Christ suffered to redeem us. We are not required to pay further penalties for sin but we will suffer for our witness. Some face persecution and even death for Christ's sake. Paul was well qualified to talk about this, but he goes on to say he has a twofold commission to fulfil, whatever the cost –

- to communicate the gospel to the Gentiles (1:27)
- to ensure that believers went on to maturity (1:28)

Paul's Struggle

This is why Paul agonised in prayer for the Colossians. He had never met them. But they were constantly on his heart and in his prayers. He wanted them to experience the unity of love and to go on to the fullest possible understanding and experience of their 'fullness' in Christ. Just as there is no stopping the progress of physical birth once the urge to deliver comes on a woman in childbirth, so Paul prays with the same urgency and intensity for the birth and growth of his converts.

Paul's Testimony

These are no mere empty words. They are backed up by his spiritual agonising. 'I am present with you in spirit and delight to see ...' Paul was an encourager, but he too was encouraged because he saw the Colossians pressing on to maturity.

Paul's Warning

And it is for us today! Beware! Don't be ensnared by wrong teaching. Be on the alert. We've been given the Word of God, His Spirit to make it clear to us, access to God in prayer, fellowship with God's children. Keep closely in touch with Him. Beware of men's theories and, however plausible, persuasive and attractive, don't be deluded by them. Press on to maturity. Can those who are concerned for your spiritual well-being say; 'I'm rejoicing and thrilled at your spiritual progress'?

Hidden Treasure

We often hear excited reports about treasures recovered from wrecked ships. At best these things are already spoilt by the ravages of time and will eventually disintegrate. In Christ we have 'eternal treasure'. Nothing that He bestows on us will be changed by time – rather they will endure through all eternity. Keep looking in the WORD for all these spiritual treasures. Draw continually on your heavenly bank account. It will never dry up. Look up Ephesians 2:7; I Corinthians 1:30; I Timothy 6:17; Colossians 3:16 then search for more!

A Challenge
Has this week's study added to your knowledge of prayer? Are you discovering that God needs more intercessors like Paul? Are you asking God to burden your heart with the needs of others? Learn from Paul and ask God to give you the grace to put prayer into practice. Paul was EARNEST, CONSISTENT, PERSISTENT and SPECIFIC in his prayers. He prayed till it hurt! Remember, someone is praying you on to maturity. Thank God for that and pray expectantly for others.

STUDY 4
MATURE IN CHRIST

QUESTIONS

DAY 1 *Colossians 2:6; James 2:19.*
a) Does believing the truth **about** Christ make us Christians?
b) What do you understand by 'receiving Christ'?

DAY 2 *Colossians 2:6; Romans 12:1, 2.*
What do you think is the difference between acknowledging Christ as Saviour and as Lord. Discuss the difference (Luke 6:46).

DAY 3 *Colossians 2:6; 1 Corinthians 6:19, 20.*
a) Why **should** Christ be Lord of our lives?
b) Discuss how His Lordship will cut across our natural outlook.

DAY 4 *Colossians 2:6, 7.*
a) Can you pick out steps of Christian progression here?
b) Read Psalm 1:1-3 and discuss the results of being rooted deeply in Christ.

DAY 5 *Colossians 2:8 (see v. 4 too!).*
a) What 'extras' were being thrown in which would weaken the church?
b) Discuss these references then paraphrase your findings: 2 Corinthians 11:3; Romans 16:17, 18; Proverbs 1:10.

DAY 6 *Colossians 2:9, 10; Colossians 1:19; John 1:14-16.*
a) How is Christ described in these verses?
b) How do I personally benefit from this?

DAY 7 *Colossians 2:11-15 (read in several translations).*
List the things that have happened to those who are 'in Him'.

Memorise Colossians 2:9, 10.

NOTES

BEGIN

New life in Christ doesn't just happen! Believing about Him doesn't change me. But when CHRIST dwells in my heart by FAITH I become a CHRISTIAN. I am ALIVE FOREVER IN CHRIST. Now I can GROW!

GO ON

How? Exactly as I began. I believed Christ died for me. I accepted the new life He purchased for me. Christ is the SOURCE of my new life. I received Him by FAITH. He continues to be my life (Col. 3:3, 4). In this confidence I WALK ON. I start in FAITH. I GO ON in FAITH. I finish in FAITH. (Paul says this in 2 Tim. 4:7.) He SAVES and KEEPS!

GROW

How? Put your roots down more deeply into Christ. Put into practice all He teaches you in His Word. All the ingredients for spiritual growth are in Him. We've been placed in the right environment for growth so keep growing (see Luke 2:51, 52 for the reason why Jesus grew!)

BEWARE

Another warning not to be side-tracked by wrong teaching or being caught up with the passing things of time. Keep your priorities right. Conforming to the world takes the sharp edge off your Christian witness and Christian happiness. Remember Jesus is the author and finisher of your faith!

REALISE

Christ is filled with God! The Christian is filled with Christ. This little bit of clay called 'me' contains all the power of God. Let's encourage one another to live in the full realisation of this tremendous truth. The devil may tempt us to FEEL empty, weak, alone. Send him packing. Tell him he's a liar. Tell him it doesn't matter how you feel, you KNOW that you are BEING CONTINUALLY FILLED WITH CHRIST. Jesus is everything you need.

One writer puts this truth of Christian maturity very clearly:

'Our part is not PRODUCTION, but RECEPTION of our life in Christ.

This entails Bible-based fact finding –

explicit FAITH in Him and His purpose for us –
patient TRUST while He takes us through the PROCESS involved.

No believer ever FELL into MATURITY even although he IS MATURE IN CHRIST.

Spiritual growth necessitates HEART HUNGER for the Lord,
DETERMINATION based on ASSURANCE, plus meditation and thought –
We can never come to a FULL REALISATION of our SPIRITUAL POSSESSIONS
through a SUPERFICIAL UNDERSTANDING OF THE WORD OF GOD ...

The development of the LIFE OF CHRIST within us is like natural growth in the
vegetable world. We do not PRODUCE growth. We grow when we place ourselves
under conditions favourable to growth.'

'Principles of Spiritual Growth' by Miles J. Stanford
(Back to the Bible Publication)

STUDY 5
IT'S NOT DO OR DON'T BUT DONE!

QUESTIONS

DAY 1 *Colossians 2:16-19; Ephesians 4:15, 16.*
a) What do these verses warn us against?
b) How could we fall into this trap?

DAY 2 *Colossians 2:20-23; Galatians 5:1; Ephesians 2:15.*
a) Read the Colossian references in several translations and put verse 20 into your own words.
b) What is Paul continually telling his converts to do?

DAY 3 *Colossians 3:1, 2.*
a) Where is Christ now?
b) Where then should our whole interest be centred?

DAY 4 *Colossians 3:3; Romans 6:11.*
a) How can we be 'dead' and 'alive' at the same time?
b) Look at yesterday's work. Think of ways we can encourage one another to obey verses 1 and 2.

DAY 5 *1 Peter 2:24; Galatians 2:19, 20; Colossians 2:20.*
a) What three things no longer have any power over the Christian?
b) Discuss what this means in every-day Christian living.

DAY 6 *Colossians 3:4; 1 John 3:2.*
a) How do we know that we shall one day see Christ?
b) What will happen to us when Christ comes again?

DAY 7 *Colossians 2:19; Ephesians 4:13-16.*
a) When Christ is acknowledged as Head what happens to the church?
b) What characteristic of Christ predominates?

Memorise Colossians 3:1-4. You won't regret it.

DO's and DON'Ts

The Jews were conditioned to the law, feasts, special rites and significant days. It was difficult for them to accept that in Christ ALONE was salvation to be found. Traditionalists and legalists, they brought pressure to bear on Christian converts to conform to the law as well as trusting Christ. This teaching could bring confusion and bondage on young Christians. The Bible tells us that 'Christ is the end of the law ... for everyone who believes' (Rom. 10:4). The law is no longer binding upon those who rest in the righteousness of Christ.

Stop! Think of some of the subtle pressures which are put upon Christians today to CONFORM. It might surprise you if you made a list of some of the 'Christian' things you do and why you do them!

DONE

When Jesus died on the cross He said 'It is finished'. His Father's heart was satisfied. Sin had been dealt with. Satan and death were vanquished. Every believer was justified. Eternal life was secured for us. There is nothing left for us to do but ACCEPT what He has DONE.

"Tis done, the great transaction's done; I am my Lord's and He is mine.'

UNION

This theme comes in like a refrain in Paul's writings. He explains it in different words, but constantly reminds us 'We died with Christ', 'We are risen with Christ', 'We are seated in Heavenly places in Christ'. He EXPECTS his converts to be setting their hearts on eternal realities and to be putting less and less value on material things. He encourages us with the glorious hope that when Christ appears we shall appear with Him, sharing His triumph and glory. He wants us to realise NOW that we are ETERNALLY UNITED WITH CHRIST and TO ENJOY ALL that relationship brings.

INCREASE

With the concept of UNION Paul emphasises Christ's HEADSHIP (Col. 1:18; 2:19; Eph. 4:13-16, etc.). The head controls. If someone has a head injury or brain lesion it is obvious from the fact that parts of the body are not functioning properly. When Christ is in full control of His body it grows and functions as it should. One day His whole body is going to be presented MATURE and COMPLETE in Him. Notice, too, the priority of LOVE in Christ's relationship to His body. When the members of His body manifest LOVE one towards the other, the whole church grows (Eph. 4:15, 16).

STUDY 6

A WHOLE NEW LIFE!

QUESTIONS

DAY 1 *Read chapter 3:1-17 in several translations.*
List all the things Christians are told to do in these verses.

DAY 2 *Colossians 3:5; Romans 8:12-14.*
a) Does God save us, then leave us to battle our own way through?
b) How is a covetous person described here?

DAY 3 *Colossians 3:5, 6; Romans 1:18.*
a) On what does God vent His wrath?
b) Read Romans 2:1-11; Hebrews 10:23-31; Revelation 11:18; 16:1-21. Discuss what you have discovered about the wrath of God.

DAY 4 a) *Ephesians 5:6*   God's wrath will come on whom?
b) *John 3:36*   God's wrath will remain where?
c) *Psalm 103:8-14*   God's .... outweighs His wrath.

DAY 5 *I Thessalonians 1:10; Colossians 3:7-10.*
a) Who delivers us from the wrath of God?
b) What marks us out as delivered people?

DAY 6 *Colossians 3:5-14.*
a) Can you list some of the things you have 'put to death'?
b) Are there other things that should go? What are you doing about them?

DAY 7 *Read Colossians 3:13-17.*
Discuss: How should we act towards those who hurt us?
What happens when God's love rules in our heart?
What should control our hearts?
What will enrich our lives?
How should the word of God affect our attitudes?
What should be our constant desire?

Memorise Colossians 3:17.

Eternal life – NOW

Really? Yes. And in heaven too! The Christian has heaven in his heart right now. I remember saying to an older Christian when I was still a very new one: 'Why is it God seems to say "no" to the things I want most?' It took me some time to believe that God was taking away the 'lesser' things of my limited desires to give me the 'greater' things that He desired for me. Often when we do earnestly pray for blessing in a certain area we seem to experience the opposite! So when we pray for PATIENCE it doesn't just fall from heaven the way we expect. God sends us TRIBULATION. Why? Because as we cope with tribulation God teaches us patience (Rom. 5:3). I discovered that these seeming trials were really stepping-stones into God's fuller purposes. By a process of 'dying out' to self-pleasing and choosing, I was becoming more Christ-centred. The more this happened the more I wanted it to happen! Paul experienced this exchanged life to the full and could say and mean it: 'For to me to live IS Christ' (Phil. 1:21).

Defeat

Yes. Christians can live in defeat. There seems to be a big gap between how I actually live and the potential victory there is for me in Christ. The truth of the matter is, that the more I want to be like Him, the more conscious I become of the 'grave-clothes' of my old existence (Gal. 5:17). God has given us healthy bodily appetites. To exercise these is my right, but to over-exercise them results in lust or excess as the Bible says (Jas. 1:13-15). List the things that beat you: Tongue (How do I use it?): Appetite (Does it rule me?): Temper (Is it controlled?): Sex (Indulged wrongly this becomes lust): Covetousness (Greed is described as idolatry which means worshipping THINGS instead of God). If we seek to 'put to death' these things which mar the image of God in us, we will know Christ's overcoming power in our lives. Colossians 3:12-17 lists the Christlike qualities which develop when we yield up our old ways to Christ's control.

Victory

Here is the Biblical recipe. It is a NO-FAIL one.

RECOGNISE the enemy can't do anything about your being a Christian. But he does want to cripple your Christian walk (1 Pet. 5:8).

RESIST, withstand, refuse (claiming the promises of God's Word) the enemy's attempts to inject unbelief into your heart, evil thoughts into your mind, dejection into your spirit. He will get the picture and 'flee from you' (Jas. 4:7).

RELY totally on the victory Christ has won. He IS the Conqueror He HAS defeated Satan. You ARE His child (Rev. 12:11). Christ is FILLED with God. You are FILLED with Christ. Remember?

Recognise! Resist! Rely!

A new outfit!
Everyone loves a new rig-out! Paul tells us to put on the beautiful garments of salvation Christ has provided for us (Col. 3:12). See what the Bible says about clothing:

Luke 24:49; I Peter 5:5; 2 Chronicles 6:41. You can discover much more. The children of the King of Kings are the best dressed people on earth!

And it doesn't cost them a penny!

STUDY 7
REWARDING RELATIONSHIPS

QUESTIONS

DAY 1 *Colossians 3:18–4:1 (Read in several translations).*
a) List the people to whom instructions are given here.
b) What supreme relationship governs our attitude to others?

DAY 2 *Colossians 3:18–4:1; Ephesians 5:23; 1 Peter 3:1-6.*
a) What relationship should the husband have to his wife?
b) What attitude should a wife have to her husband? Even if he is not a Christian?

DAY 3 *Genesis 3:16; 1 Corinthians 11:3; 1 Corinthians 15:27-28; Philippians 2:7-9.*
a) What do these verses tell us about biblical headship?
b) Look up Genesis 3:16; Ephesians 5:21-24; Philippians 2:7-9; 1 Peter 5:5. Discuss what you have discovered about biblical submission.

DAY 4 *Colossians 3:19; Ephesians 5:25, 28, 29, 33.*
a) What is basic to the proper exercising of both authority and submission?
b) Describe the prescribed quality of a man's love for his wife.

DAY 5 *Colossians 3:19; 1 Peter 3:7; 1 Corinthians 13:4-8. (Read in several translations.)*
a) What happens when a husband has a wrong attitude to his wife?
b) Are you lacking in love? What are you going to do about it?

DAY 6 *Colossians 3:20, 21; Ephesians 6:1-4.*
a) Why should children obey their parents?
b) What have fathers (1) to do (2) not to do to their children?

QUESTIONS (contd.)

DAY 7 *Colossians 3:22–4:1; Ephesians 6:5-9.*
a) How are bosses and their employees to relate to one another? Make a list of DO's and DON'Ts for both categories (use the Ephesians verses).
b) Look up 2 Chronicles 31:21 and see what you can discover about Hezekiah!

Memorise Colossians 3:23, 24.

This is a most important study, especially as our society in general disregards the sanctity of marriage and the trend has been towards a severe 'generation gap'. As Christians we should do everything possible to understand and operate on biblical principles in family relationships. Ask your leader for book titles available on different angles of Christian family living.

BASIC RELATIONSHIPS,
Marital relationships and interpersonal relationships should be patterned on Christ's relationship with His Bride, the Church. Paul has already discussed (Col. 3:12-15) the attitudes which should characterise the members of Christ's body and now goes on to apply this to specific relationships. These are regularised when we walk in vital outworking of our 'Union with Christ'.

EACH FOR THE OTHER
God can fill our hearts with a compassion that yearns for the well-being of others. Read Genesis 43:30 and see how Joseph reacted, not in justifiable hatred, but in love. Jeremiah 30:20 shows God yearning over His wayward children. True humility puts OTHERS before SELF! A forgiving spirit paves the way to peace. LOVE (the mark of spiritual maturity, see I John 4:12) is the greatest binding force on earth (I Pet. 4:8).

HUSBAND AND WIFE
A husband stands in relationship to his wife as Christ does to the Church. Christ's headship resulted from His voluntary humbling of Himself. He sacrificed Himself that He might bestow upon His bride His eternal love and riches. A husband's love is but a shadow of Christ's love. But his wife's submission (a reflection of her submission to Christ) is a biblical demand whether her husband patterns his authority on Christ's and earnestly lives for her well-being or not! God's command is that the husband is to love her as he loves his own body. Note that the wife's part, submission, is reflexive! Submission obtained by force is not submission. The Greek word means 'a voluntary placing of oneself under another'. Just as the love of Christ causes us to capitulate to Christ, so should a husband's love call forth this reaction from his partner. The submissive wife can be the means of her unsaved partner's salvation!

PARENT AND CHILD
Children brought up in a Christian home should obey their parents (Eph. 6:1) not only because God tells them to, but also out of respect for those who gave them life, but it doesn't always work out this way. Why not? There are two sides to this question. Scripture sets out the basics for the Christian family. Even Christ, the

Son of God, was subject to His earthly parents (Luke 2:51) and was accordingly blessed. Somewhere along the line, as scriptural principles are taught and hearts changed, legal obedience should be replaced by a relationship of deference and love. Exodus 20:12 is a promise for children, but how much greater the blessing when obedience is voluntary and not demanded. Parents are to earn this love-response by not making unreasonable demands, not stirring to anger and by a ministry of encouragement. Discipline, train and reprove in the Spirit of the Lord (Eph. 6:4). See also Deuteronomy 6:7; Proverbs 22:6; Hebrews 12:6-11.

THE WORK FORCE
All men are set free in Christ (1 Cor. 7:22, 23) and requested to serve one another in love (Gal. 5:13). Ideally this should be the atmosphere in which people work. But how many work situations are ideal? Even when Christians work in a non-Christian environment they are to exercise Christian grace and attitudes.

The Christian employee can serve a non-Christian boss by doing the job as unto the Lord. That entails thoroughness, consistency, respect, deference – all the Christian qualities that he would have towards fellow Christian.

The Christian boss has to recognise that the equality of faith takes priority over rank or distinction and he is to maintain a wholly Christian attitude desiring his employees' highest good.

Two thoughts to ponder:

In my **marriage relationship** am I praying and working towards the goal of seeing the maximum spiritual potential achieved in my partner?

In my concept of **love** do I take into account that Christ loved me and gave Himself for me when my relationship with Him was broken by sin?

'Christ drew me to Himself not with threats, insult and terror, but by tenderness, complete self-giving and totally unmerited love. A husband is already united to his wife when he is asked to endure for her sake, suffering if need be that she be preserved. He looks for a return of human love and responsiveness. There is no human bond so binding as this. It is the basis of all human joy. It is worth striving for' (extract – author unknown).

STUDY 8

SHARING – CARING – PRAYING

QUESTIONS

DAY 1 *Colossians 4:2; Luke 11:5-10.*
a) What three important things does verse 2 tell us about prayer?
b) What do the Luke verses tell us about persistence in prayer?

DAY 2 *Colossians 4:3, 4.*
a) Who is speaking in verse 3 and why does he say 'us'?
b) How specific were the Colossians to be in prayer for them?

DAY 3 *Colossians 4:5, 6.*
a) Discuss ways we can 'make the most of our time' (RSV).
b) What is said here about the way we TALK and ACT?

DAY 4 *Colossians 4:2; Matthew 18:19, 20.*
a) Do you find it difficult to spend time alone in prayer?
b) Are there any benefits from praying with others?

DAY 5 *Colossians 4:7, 8.*
a) Paul says three things about Tychicus here. What are they?
b) Why is Tychicus visiting the Colossians?

DAY 6 *Colossians 4:9.*
a) Who was to accompany Tychicus?
b) Where did he come from?

DAY 7 *Colossians 1:3, 9-12.*
a) Look back at STUDY 1, DAY 4 and DAY 7, also STUDY 3, DAY 4. Are you learning lessons on prayer?
b) Why don't you share prayer problems and victories then pray for each other?

Memorise Colossians 4:6.

NOTES

SHARE

Have you noticed how helpful it is when people share their joys and problems in the study group? In a very real way we can identify with each other because we all face similar problems and trials and have mutual reasons for rejoicing. 'Identification' is a theme which has been running through these studies. We are identified with Christ in His death and resurrection. We need to remind ourselves that we can only identify with Him because He was first willing to come to earth and identify with us. He even 'became sin' for us. Read Philippians 2:7, 8 and Hebrews 4:15. Jesus truly shared our human lot. He understands us through and through. This study has reminded us that we are members 'one of another' and as such we should fully identify with one another. That means weeping with those who are sorrowful and rejoicing with those who are happy (Rom. 12:15).

CARE

It isn't enough just to share. We are to care. Christian love, the love of Christ coming through us (Rom. 5:5) is the key to really caring for the well-being of others. Jesus cared (loved) enough to die for us. How much time, energy, love, patience, prayer do you expend on others who are 'going through the mill'? Sometimes we feel we have no more to give, we are utterly drained as we seek to stand with others. It is then that we realise more fully that human love, wisdom and strength are not enough. Like Paul we have to draw on Christ's resources (Phil. 4:13).

A missionary who served in South America tells how she went out full of high hope to share the love of Jesus with these people whom God had called her to serve. But she found them anything but lovable! She couldn't get used to their obnoxious habits and filthy ways. She found their language difficult. What could she do? Go home a failure? No, she told the Lord He would have to be her resource and enabling in this impossible situation. Only then could she love these people – with the love of God. God's love did come through. It came through so effectively that the national woman who worked with her in the kitchen became a Christian before that missionary could speak a word of her language!

PRAYER

If we share and care, the outcome should be prayer. Prayer is the power-line. Prayer releases the power of God in a situation. We don't know how this works, but it does. Prayer brings the pray-er's heart into line with what God wants. It brings the pray-er to a knowledge of God's will. It enables the pray-er to claim God's promises. It encourages the pray-er to faith in what God will do. Are you learning the ABC's of prayer?

Ask in faith (Matt. 21:22)
Ask according to God's will (1 John 5:14, 15)
Ask in Jesus' Name, that is, in His authority (John 14:13, 14)
Pray with a partner (Matt. 18:19. How about husband and wife?)
Ask earnestly and persistently (Eph. 6:18)
Ask specifically (Mark 10:51)

Read about Daniel. He prayed and triumphed (Dan. 6). He said: 'So I turned to the Lord God' (Dan. 9:3).

We have the same wonder-working God. We have a fuller access – through Christ.

Let's prove Him too.

One Christ
   One Cross
      One sacrifice
       One priest
        One altar
          One temple for us all
            One Spirit in whose common bond we meet
            One Father on whose name we call
            One Mercy seat ...

STUDY 9

DON'T COOL OFF!

QUESTIONS

DAY 1 *Colossians 4:2-8.*
a) How would you describe Paul's attitude to others?
b) How did he want the Colossian Christians to live?

DAY 2 *Colossians 4:7-14, 17.*
a) Did Paul's fellow-workers manifest a similar attitude?
b) Why do you think Paul needed to send this special message to Archippus?

DAY 3 a) What made our salvation possible (John 3:16)?
b) What motivates us to reach out to others (2 Cor. 5:14, 15,20)?
c) When are we to witness to others (1 Pet. 3:15)?
d) Why are we to witness to others (1 John 1:3)?

DAY 4 *Colossians 4:12.*
a) How did Epaphras pray for the Colossians?
b) Put into your own words Epaphras' desire for the Colossians.

DAY 5 *Colossians 4:12; 1:9 (refer to STUDY 1, DAY 5).*
a) Is this your desire for yourself and your friends?
b) How can God's purposes be fully implemented in our lives?

DAY 6 *Colossians 4:7-17.*
a) List Paul's friends mentioned in these verses.
b) What do you discover about each of them from this chapter?

DAY 7 *Colossians 4:16; Revelation 3:13-22.*
a) What was the church like at Laodicea?
b) Were Paul's epistles only for the specific churches he wrote to?
Why or why not?

Memorise Colossians 4:17b and Revelation 3:21, 22.

NOTES

Near the end of Colossians Paul sends Christian greetings to an obviously thriving church at Laodicea. Later, in Revelation 3:14-22 we read about this church again. But now it is very different. What had happened?

The city had been ravaged by an earthquake in AD 61, but the people showed themselves to be resourceful and self-sufficient by rebuilding it without the aid of the then-ruling Nero.

Prosperity marked its development and was largely the result of its medical school (which produced a world famous eye ointment apparently), its trade in BLACK wool and its effective banking system. In the midst of this great affluence and materialism, the church had lost its cutting edge for God. It had COOLED OFF or switched into NEUTRAL spiritually. What a difference between Laodicea and Smyrna which was materially poor, but spiritually rich (Rev. 2:9).

The sad thing was that the Laodiceans were unaware of their spiritual poverty. Often there is more hope for the OPENLY ANTAGONISTIC than for the COOLY INDIFFERENT. God finds neutrality unacceptable.

Look up Joshua 24:15 – Joshua said, 'Choose for yourselves this day whom you will serve' and in I Kings 18:21 – Elijah said 'How long will you waver between two opinions?'

In Hebrews 10:28, 29 we find judgment being passed on those who take lightly Christ's sacrifice and whose lives are an insult to a holy God.

What is God saying to the Laodicean church in Revelation 3:14-22?

First, He assesses their spiritual life
'Let all who can hear listen to what My spirit is saying' (v. 13 LB).
'I know you well. You are neither HOT nor COLD. I wish you were one way or the other' (v. 15).
'Since you are merely LUKEWARM I will spit you out of my mouth' (v. 16).
'You say "I am rich; I have everything I want; I don't need a thing!" I say you are SPIRITUALLY WRETCHED, MISERABLE, POOR, BLIND, NAKED' (v. 17).

Then He tells them how to remedy the problem
'My advice is buy purified gold from Me only then will you be truly rich' (3:18). [See what I Pet. 1:7 says.]
'Purchase from Me white garments, clean, pure, so you won't be naked and ashamed' (3:18). [See Isa. 61:10; Rev. 19:8.]
'Get eye medicine from Me to heal your eyes and restore your sight' (3:18). [See John 8:12; 9:39; 2 Cor. 3:14-18.]
'I continually discipline and correct everyone I love, so I will have to punish

you unless you turn from your indifference and become enthusiastic about the things of God' (3:19).

'Look, I'm standing knocking, waiting, ready to come so that we can have fellowship together. Everyone who conquers (Rom. 8:37; Rev. 6:2) will sit beside Me on My throne just as I took My place with My Father on His throne when I had conquered' (3:20, 21).

Has someone a Living or Good News Bible at hand? Read Hebrews 3:13-19. It is a sobering thought to realise that any of us can COOL OFF SPIRITUALLY. Many things can come in to make our hearts grow cold –

- Being self-satisfied
- Being self-sufficient
- Letting unbelief take over
- Loving things better than we love the Lord
- Being unloving
- Neglecting prayer, fellowship and God's Word.

You can think of many more I'm sure. How about helping each other in areas where we are defaulting?

'Speak to each other about these things EVERY DAY' (Heb. 3:13).
'Encourage and warn each other as the day of the Lord's coming draws near' (Heb. 10:25).

Moffat's translation of Romans 12:11 gives us the message very neatly:

Never let your ZEAL flag...
    Maintain your SPIRITUAL GLOW...
        SERVE THE LORD.

STUDY 10

THE RUNAWAY!

QUESTIONS

DAY 1 *Philemon vv. 1-25.*
a) List all the people mentioned in this letter.
b) How many have you heard of before and what do you know about them?

DAY 2 *Philemon vv. 1-5; Colossians 4:17.*
a) What can you discover about Philemon, Apphia and Archippus from these verses?
b) Do you see Paul's 'major' ministry to the church again? What is it?

DAY 3 *Philemon vv. 6-9.*
a) What does Paul pray for Philemon and his fellow Christians?
b) What brings Paul joy and comfort?
c) Instead of using his authority as an older apostle, how does he exhort Philemon?

DAY 4 *Philemon vv. 10-13; Colossians 4:9.*
a) Have you discovered anything about Onesimus from these verses?
b) What did Paul very much want to do with Onesimus?

DAY 5 *Philemon vv. 14-16; 1 Timothy 6:2.*
a) How does Paul interpret Philemon's temporary loss of his slave?
b) Describe the new relationship they could now have.

DAY 6 *Philemon vv. 17-19.*
a) How does Paul propose to settle Onesimus' debt to Philemon?
b) What does Philemon owe to Paul?

DAY 7 *Philemon vv. 20-25.*
a) How highly did Paul rate Philemon's character?
b) What did Paul ask Philemon to do for him and why?

NOTES

Paul certainly lived in the reality that he was FILLED with God. Over and over again we see how God's purposes came through him, even in the most adverse situations and impossible places – like prison!

In this brief letter we discover that a runaway slave came under his influence. He became a Christian. Not only was he converted, but obviously he had become stabilised in his faith. (Philem. v. 11 says 'useful' which indicates a degree of spiritual maturity).

In Paul's actions here we see again the outstanding quality of Christian love. The love which constrained Paul to minister to Onesimus causes him to plead with Philemon for reconciliation. He appeals to the love of Christ in Philemon, knowing that restoration on that basis would be sure to work out.

Paul could easily have felt he had a 'right' to keep this new son in the faith as a companion and helper. But he knew the most profitable thing for both Philemon and Onesimus would be a healed relationship. In some small way this reflects the love of the Lord Jesus who stripped Himself of His 'rights' that we (defaulters like Onesimus!) might be restored to God.

Would Onesimus be willing to go back and 'face the music'? That would surely test his Christian character. Would Philemon be willing to forgive and forget? Have you discovered how important it is once you are 'squared up' with God, to do everything humanly possible to put things right with people you have wronged? It is hard, but it pays off and is the scriptural pattern (see Matt. 5:23, 24).

What made Onesimus a thief? Why did he run away? Why should Philemon, a good Christian master be treated in this way? Did he question God and say, 'Why me, God? What have I done to merit this packet?' How did it all work out?

Many Christian parents have had cause to question God when a child who has been trained to love God 'kicks over the traces'. Take heart! In a literal translation from the Greek, Romans 8:28 says, 'And we know that to the (ones) loving God, God works together all things for good to the ones being called according to (God's) purposes. God encourages us to hold on to His promises during these times of darkness and testing.

PRAYER! Here it is again. Paul thanking God for his fellow Christians, rejoicing in their work and witness, praying they will effectively communicate the gospel. Paul prays for himself something to which God may have said 'No'.

'I trust I will be able to come to you...' (v. 22). We have no record of Paul's release. We don't know if he ever saw his friends again. We do know he was prepared for possible death although he mused, 'I'm torn in two. I want to stay with you, yet it would be far better to go and be with Christ' (Phil. 1:23).

His one desire was to magnify Christ, whether by life or death and he said ...

'For to me, to LIVE IS CHRIST and to DIE IS GAIN'. Can you say this too?

For me to live is Christ, to die is gain,
To hold His hand, and walk His narrow way.
There is no peace, no joy, no thrill
Like walking in His will ...
For me to LIVE IS CHRIST
... TO DIE IS GAIN.

ANSWER GUIDE

The following pages contain an Answer Guide. It is recommended that answers to the questions be attempted before turning to this guide. It is only a guide and the answers given should not be treated as exhaustive.

GUIDE TO INTRODUCTORY STUDY

The introductory study to this series should give the group a good foundation to build on. Be sure you can locate the places mentioned on the map and point out how people from all around Jerusalem had reasonable access to the city both by land and sea.

In the introduction:

The first section shows that the gospel could have reached Colossae either through a convert from Ephesus or some area of Phrygia after Paul's visits. He had preached the gospel widely there. Also, Phrygians (there could have been some from Laodicea) were in Jerusalem at Pentecost and could have carried the Good News back home.

Section two is to emphasise the importance of basing all our faith on Christ and His Word and to show how the introduction of man's interpretation of Scripture can adulterate the pure Word of God and lead people astray. Stress the point that the important thing is not 'I think...' but what the Bible says. It is so important that we rely on the Spirit of God to enlighten us (I Cor. 2:10; Matt. 16:17; Luke 10:21) and realise the safeguards of belonging to a sound church where the truths and principles of the Word of God are taught and lived out.

Section three will need little explanation. Christ is seen as the sole and total answer to our every need. He is 'Jesus the Crucified, far above all'. It would be good to pause at this point and praise God together that 'all the fulness of the Godhead dwells in Jesus and we are complete in Him'.

GUIDE TO STUDY 1

DAY 1   a) Paul wrote this letter to the members of the church at Colossae.
b) Timothy, one of Paul's converts, had a Greek father and Jewish mother. He was Paul's companion in ministry, and was beloved as a spiritual 'son'.

DAY 2   a) 'Apostle' means a devoted follower or advocate commissioned, and sent by, and dedicated to ... in the Bible context, Christ.
b) Paul testifies he was 'called' by Jesus Christ to be an apostle.
c) When God redeems us to Himself He calls each of us to be His loving and devoted servants and witnesses.

DAY 3   a) Paul praised God for their faith (v. 4), love (vv. 4, 8) and hope (v. 5).
b) Epaphras was a Colossian Christian who had founded and now ministered to the church there.

DAY 4   a) Constantly.
b) Paul prayed that the Colossians might be filled with wisdom and knowledge. They were to show by the way they lived that they were Christians. They would do this by relying on Christ's strength (see Eph. 3:16).

DAY 5   a) Read the verses in several translations. Have various ones give their paraphrasing.
b) We discover His will when we yield fully to Him and constantly allow Him to take rightful control of our lives. This only happens when we truly WANT and ASK for GOD'S WAY rather than determinedly taking our OWN WAY.

DAY 6   a) While we were still sinners Christ died for us (Rom. 5:8). When we receive Christ and become God's children we are delivered from Satan's bondage. (See Rev. 12:10, 11).
b) Personal.

DAY 7   a) Personal.
b) Note that the prayer points in verses 9-12 can be broken down to specifics. Encourage the group to share areas of need in their prayer life. Have a session of prayer for each other either in small groups or all together.

GUIDE TO STUDY 2

DAY 1 a) From the control of SIN, SATAN AND HELL.
b) God has brought us into the Kingdom of His Son – the Kingdom of Light.

DAY 2 a) Jesus Christ reveals to us what God is like – Jesus is exactly like His Father.
b) Jesus has ALWAYS existed. He is from everlasting to everlasting!

DAY 3 a) The universe was created by Christ.
b) The whole of creation is held together by the power of the Son of God.

DAY 4 a) The Church is the body of Christ, i.e. each Christian is part of His body.
b) Christ is Head and Source of the body – His Church.

DAY 5 a) We were alienated from God by sin.
b) Christ's sacrifice was the only basis upon which God could cleanse us from sin. Jesus is the ONLY WAY to God. His atoning work is not only sufficient for our salvation, but by it He can present us FAULTLESS to God.

DAY 6 a) To cleanse and separate us from sin, make us righteous before God and bring us into fellowship with God.
b) Christ's work becomes effective in my life when I BELIEVE He died for me personally and RELY wholly on Him for my salvation.

DAY 7 a) If we take our eyes off Christ and His promises the devil can tempt us to DOUBT.
b) The hope of one day being in God's presence but we are not to DRAW BACK, but KEEP BELIEVING (1 Pet. 1:9).

GUIDE TO STUDY 3

DAY 1
a) Jesus suffered for our SALVATION. The apostles suffered for their FAITH IN CHRIST.
b) All Christians suffer in some measure for their faith (Matt. 5:11, 12; Heb. 10:34; Heb. 11:24-26; Rom. 8:18, etc.).

DAY 2
a) To preach the gospel to all men in general but NON-JEWS in particular (Acts 26:17, 18).
b) Christ died for our sins (fulfilling Isa. 53) but triumphed over sin and death.

DAY 3
a) 2 Corinthians 3:12-14 reminds us that in Old Testament days the people could not go into the Holy Place where God presenced Himself. Now, through Christ, believers can draw near to God.
b) Paul WARNS men that they need to be SAVED and INSTRUCTS believers that they might become MATURE in Christ (1 Cor. 15:1; 2 Cor. 11:2).

DAY 4
a) The words LABOUR, STRUGGLE, STRIVE, CONFLICT (different in different translations) indicate that Paul was so 'sold out' in his task that he positively LABOURED or AGONISED in prayer.
b) God was the source of his power and enabling (v. 29).

DAY 5
a) Their SPIRITUAL WELL-BEING (as against material prosperity).
b) Practical and constant application of the truths that God teaches us through His Word and by His Spirit.
c) Christian love.

DAY 6
a) All God's fullness (that includes all wisdom and knowledge) are 'hidden' in Christ.
b) All that Christ is and has are for the believer; His riches are concealed from the unbeliever.

DAY 7
a) Although Paul had never been with them he was ONE in spirit with them, strongly linked in the bond of prayer fellowship.
b) They were steadfast in their faith and their lives witnessed to Christ. They were a joy to Epaphras who obviously took the trouble to send reports of their progress back to Paul in prison.

GUIDE TO STUDY 4

DAY 1
a) Believing ABOUT doesn't change us. Believing on or in Christ does.
b) 'Receiving' speaks of personally accepting and appropriating our salvation in Christ.

DAY 2
We can selfishly want salvation and personal security by receiving Christ as Saviour but real joy and assurance results when we yield to Christ's Lordship and give Him the right to direct and control our lives. 'If He is not Lord of all, He is not Lord at all!'

DAY 3
a) Not only are we His by right of creation, but we have been redeemed from Satan and sin by His atoning sacrifice.
b) It is NATURAL to live for what we want! When Christ becomes Lord, our old SELF-CENTREDNESS is shaken. In the process of becoming CHRIST-CENTRED our priorities and values are changed and we learn to delight in Him and in His will.

DAY 4
a) As we grow in Christ we are ROOTED DOWN and BUILT UP in Him.
b) Love and obedience to God's Word ensures that our spiritual roots keep going deeper. As we draw from His rich resources our lives are enriched. Like the tree planted by the river, we flourish (and others benefit).

DAY 5
a) When men pit their human, finite wisdom against the eternal wisdom of God, biblical teaching can become adulterated and spiritual principles watered down.
b) Jewish teachers, well-meaning but wrong, taught 'Yes, have Christ, but as well you must do this or that'. In Christ alone is salvation found (Heb. 10:10).

DAY 6
a) All the power of God is embodied in Christ – He is the Head of all principality and power.
b) I am made COMPLETE (being continually filled with) in Him.

DAY 7
They have become fully identified with Him in His death and resurrection.
In His death – we die and so die out to sin.
In His life – we too are raised to New Life in Him.
'The legal decree which was against us has been set aside and completely cleared by Christ – it was nailed to the Cross' (Col. 2:14 Amplified Bible).
Because Jesus fully identified with us (became sin for us) we can fully identify with Him in His victory (we are made righteous in Him).

GUIDE TO STUDY 5

DAY 1
a) The danger of depending on 'external' standards or a human code of ethics in Christian living.
b) By failing to acknowledge Christ as our Head – only source of righteousness.

DAY 2
a) Christ, and not an external standard, is our righteousness. Knowing this sets us free from following the world's ideas of how to be a Christian.
b) Remain wholly free in Christ. Don't go back into legalism.

DAY 3
a) In Heaven, seated at God's right hand.
b) In Christ and eternal realities, not on the passing things of time (Rom. 8:6).

DAY 4
a) We die out to sin in Christ and are made eternally alive in Him. Hebrews 12:1-3 gives us the key to personal victory.
b) God has given the blessings of His Word, prayer, human comfort, fellowship and testimony to encourage us to be heaven-orientated rather than earth-orientated.

DAY 5
a) Those 'in Christ' have died out to SIN, LEGALISM and the WORLD SYSTEM.
b) We should lose the desire to deliberately sin, to attain righteousness by self-effort, to be more caught up with the world system than with spiritual progress.

DAY 6
a) The Word of God tells us He will come back in triumph.
b) We shall be like HIM!

DAY 7
a) We all – UNITEDLY – go on to maturity in Christ.
b) LOVE.

GUIDE TO STUDY 6

DAY 1   Seek and set the heart on spiritual things and values. Refuse any desire that will deflect us from being Christ-centred; be marked out as God's people by showing mercy, kindness, humility, meekness, patience, forgiveness, love. Let God's peace garrison our hearts; be thankful; live by the Word of God; use it to teach and rebuke others; use it in praise to God. Do everything in the Lord's name and for His sake.

DAY 2   a) No, by reliance on the Spirit the Christian can know constant victory.
b) As an idolater (see what the Bible says about that – Eph. 5:5).

DAY 3   a) God's wrath is on all DISOBEDIENCE, UNGODLINESS and UNRIGHTEOUSNESS.
b) Those who DELIBERATELY and HABITUALLY SIN incur His wrath.

DAY 4   a) Those who DISOBEY GOD.
b) On those who DISBELIEVE the Son of God.
c) God's MERCY outweighs His wrath.

DAY 5   a) Jesus.
b) The believer in Jesus is CHANGED from what he was into the likeness of Jesus (i.e. into the person God created him to be – see Gen. 1:26; Eph. 2:10).

DAY 6   a) When we grow in Christ old unChrist-like habits become abhorrent to us.
b) A DESIRE to be like Jesus heightens our consciousness of areas where we fall short and we should be PURPOSELY seeking to change. Share together ways in which you are changing.

DAY 7   List your findings then check with DAY 1.
Either in small groups or as a class have a time of PRAISE and PRAYER.
• Thank God for all the 'changing' He has done in each of us so far.
• TRUST Him for the 'much more' He is going to do.
Be SPECIFIC about your needs. God will answer (see what He did for the blind man when he was specific: Luke 18:41-43; and what He promises His children: John 16:24).

GUIDE TO STUDY 7

DAY 1 a) Wives, husbands, children, fathers, employers, employees.
b) When Christ is truly first and we live to please Him, other relationships come into proper perspective.

DAY 2 a) Patterned on Christ's headship over the Church, a husband is to be 'head' of his wife.
b) A wife is to be lovingly submissive as the Church is (should be!) to Jesus Christ.

DAY 3 a) We could profitably study this further now but will do it more fully in another series.
b) Meanwhile, leaders should read the notes on STUDY 7 and be ready to guide the discussion.

DAY 4 a) There must be genuine Christlike love and reverence (deference too!).
b) Just as Christ gave Himself voluntarily for the life and blessing of His Church, so a husband is to be self-giving that his wife may be all that God planned she should be.

DAY 5 a) Their prayers cannot be answered! God cannot move on behalf of someone who is disobedient to His commands (See Matt. 5:23, 24; 6:12, 14, 15).
b) Discuss what unanswered prayer could mean in every realm – husband, wife, children, others.

DAY 6 a) God tells them to! It is pleasing to Him. It prepares them for obedience to God. It paves the way to prosperity and long life. Because parents love their children and obedience is a love-response from a child.
b) Fathers are to train their children to obey God and live by His standards.
They are not to discourage them or taunt them (which stirs them to anger).

DAY 7 a) *Masters* – deal justly and fairly as your heavenly Master deals with you.
Servants – obey (not just when you are being watched) with all your heart as a sincere expression of your devotion to the Lord.
Masters – Do not threaten or be abusive. Do treat them as you want God to treat you.
Servants – Do your work as unto the Lord, with a willing heart knowing God will reward you.
b) Hezekiah did EVERYTHING wholeheartedly as unto the Lord and he PROSPERED.

GUIDE TO STUDY 8

DAY 1 a) Continue (persist), Watch (be vigilant, keep alert), Express your thankfulness.
b) The caller got what he needed because he kept asking (and believed his friend would help!).

DAY 2 a) Paul is speaking and refers to his fellow workers.
b) They were to pray for specific opportunities for Paul to witness for Christ, even in prison!

DAY 3 a) We are to be good stewards of TIME as well as everything else God gives us; that takes self-discipline!
b) We are to WALK and TALK under the control and direction of the Spirit of God.

DAY 4 a) Most people find concentration in prayer for a long time, quite difficult. Keeping a prayer list of people and requests and noting down answers helps a lot.
b) Praying with others helps us concentrate and God promises His presence and blessing in answered prayer when we pray together.

DAY 5 a) Beloved brother, faithful minister, co-worker in Christ.
b) To bring them news of Paul; to find out how they were and to encourage them.

DAY 6 a) Onesimus.
b) Probably from Colossae as he was a member of the church there.

DAY 7 a) This book encourages us all to engage in prayer and loving concern for others.
b) It is good to carry a prayer burden for others. Concern and prayer for close friends will develop in us an increasing burden for others who need Christ. Thus we can become intercessors with Christ for the world.

GUIDE TO STUDY 9

DAY 1   a) He was constantly concerned for the spiritual welfare of others.
b) In a way that would commend Christ to unbelievers.

DAY 2   a) Paul stresses their faithfulness and concern for others.
b) Was he growing a little weary, uncaring, unconcerned for others?

DAY 3   a) God's love and concern for us provided a way of salvation.
b) God's love constrains us to live for Him and reach others with His love.
c) We are to be ALWAYS ready to witness.
d) That they may also know the joy of sins forgiven and fellowship in the Lord.

DAY 4   a) 'He is always wrestling' i.e. he literally agonised in prayer for them.
b) Epaphras yearned to see the Colossian Christians 'mature and confident' in the will of God.

DAY 5   a) Personal.
b) When our minds, hearts and wills are set on God, and when our values are set on eternity rather than time, God's purposes will be fulfilled in and through us.

DAY 6   a) Tychicus, Onesimus, Aristarchus, Mark, Barnabas, Justus, Epaphras, Luke, Demas, Nympha, Archippus.
b) Underline and discuss what the verses say about each one, e.g. Nympha had a church in her home (v. 15), Barnabas (once opposed by Paul) is acknowledged as an authoritative teacher (v. 10), etc.

DAY 7   a) Revelation 3:15, 17 describe how materialistic and backslidden it was.
b) No. Every church and Christian all down the years needs all the teaching, rebuke, encouragement, etc., found in Paul's epistles. What does your church need?

GUIDE TO STUDY 10

DAY 1 a) Paul – the apostle and writer. Timothy – Paul's convert and fellow worker. Philemon, Apphia, Archippus. Epaphras – founder-member-minister in Colossae and now a fellow prisoner with Paul. Dr. Luke, writer of the gospel and Paul's companion in prison (Col. 4:14). Demas – a fellow labourer and prisoner who eventually deserted the cause (2 Tim. 4:10). Onesimus – accompanied Tychicus when he was sent to encourage the Colossians (Col. 4:9). Mark and Aristarchus.
b) Personal.

DAY 2 a) They are all believers (Philemon – fellow labourer, Apphia – beloved, Archippus – fellow soldier). They live at Colossae. Philemon uses his home for Christian fellowship (Apphia is possibly his wife and Archippus his son).
b) Paul, with a prayer burden for all, includes these Christians in his prayers.

DAY 3 a) That they may effectively communicate their faith to others.
b) Philemon and his household obviously give hospitality and minister to Christians.
c) Paul uses Christian love, not apostolic authority in his appeal to Philemon.

DAY 4 a) Onesimus was one of Paul's converts. He had obviously absconded from Philemon's service – a runaway or 'no hoper' – and somehow got to Paul in prison. Now, changed by the gospel, he was being urged by Paul to return to his master.
b) Paul would have loved to have kept him, now a beloved son in the faith, to minister to him.

DAY 5 a) Onesimus' failure had resulted in good. Out of his new relationship in Christ, could come a new and better relationship with Philemon. But would Philemon be willing to accept him?
b) Onesimus might still be a slave, but also he would be a brother in the Lord to Philemon. Would Philemon love him as Paul loved him?

DAY 6 a) Paul himself would pay back what Onesimus owed Philemon. But perhaps there would be no need for that.
b) Since Philemon obviously owed a debt of love to Paul (he had found the Saviour through Paul) he might overlook the debt incurred by Onesimus.

DAY 7 a) Paul was confident that Philemon would delight his heart by receiving Onesimus back and giving him a Christian welcome.
b) Paul obviously felt that the prayers of his friends would be answered and that he would be restored to them so he asked Philemon to get ready for his coming.

THE WORD WORLDWIDE

We first heard of WORD WORLDWIDE over 20 years ago when Marie Dinnen, its founder, shared excitedly about the wonderful way ministry to one needy woman had exploded to touch many lives. It was great to see the Word of God being made central in the lives of thousands of men and women, then to witness the life-changing results of them applying the Word to their circumstances. Over the years the vision for WORD WORLDWIDE has not dimmed in the hearts of those who are involved in this ministry. God is still at work through His Word and in today's self-seeking society, the Word is even more relevant to those who desire true meaning and purpose in life. WORD WORLDWIDE is a ministry of WEC International, an interdenominational missionary society, whose sole purpose is to see Christ known, loved and worshipped by all, particularly those who have yet to hear of His wonderful name. This ministry is a vital part of our work and we warmly recommend the WORD WORLDWIDE 'Geared for Growth' Bible studies to you. We know that as you study His Word you will be enriched in your personal walk with Christ. It is our hope that as you are blessed through these studies, you will find opportunities to help others discover a personal relationship with Jesus. As a mission we would encourage you to work with us to make Christ known to the ends of the earth.

Stewart and Jean Moulds – British Directors, **WEC International**.

A full list of over 50 'Geared for Growth' studies can be obtained from:

ENGLAND   John and Ann Edwards
5 Louvain Terrace, Hetton-le-Hole, Tyne & Wear, DH5 9PP
Tel. 0191 5262803 Email: rhysjohn.edwards@virgin.net

IRELAND   Steffney Preston
33 Harcourts Hill, Portadown, Craigavon, N. Ireland, BT62 3RE
Tel. 028 3833 7844 Email: sa.preston@talk21.com

SCOTLAND Margaret Halliday
10 Douglas Drive, Newton Mearns, Glasgow, G77 6HR
Tel. 0141 639 8695 Email: m.halliday@ntlworld.com

WALES   William and Eirian Edwards
Penlan Uchaf, Carmarthen Road, Kidwelly, Carms., SA17 5AF
Tel. 01554 890423 Email: Penlan.uchaf@farming.co.uk

UK CO-ORDINATOR
Anne Jenkins
2 Windermere Road, Carnforth, Lancs., LA5 9AR
Tel. 01524 734797 Email: anne@jenkins.abelgratis.com

UK Website: www.wordworldwide.org.uk

Christian Focus Publications

publishes books for all ages

Our mission statement –

STAYING FAITHFUL

In dependence upon God we seek to help make His infallible word, the Bible, relevant. Our aim is to ensure that the Lord Jesus Christ is presented as the only hope to obtain forgiveness of sin, live a useful life and look forward to heaven with Him.

REACHING OUT

Christ's last command requires us to reach out to our world with His gospel. We seek to help fulfill that by publishing books that point people towards Jesus and help them to develop a Christ-like maturity. We aim to equip all levels of readers for life, work, ministry and mission.

Books in our adult range are published in three imprints.

Christian Focus contains popular works including biographies, commentaries, basic doctrine, and Christian living. Our children's books are also published in this imprint.

Mentor focuses on books written at a level suitable for Bible College and seminary students, pastors, and other serious readers. The imprint includes commentaries, doctrinal studies, examination of current issues, and church history.

Christian Heritage contains classic writings from the past.

For details of our titles visit us on our website
www.christianfocus.com

ISBN 0 908067 21 6

Copyright © WEC International

Published in 2002 by
Christian Focus Publications, Geanies House,
Fearn, Ross-shire, IV20 ITW, Scotland
and
WEC International, Bulstrode, Oxford Road,
Gerrards Cross, Bucks, SL9 8SZ

Cover design by Alister MacInnes

Printed and bound by J.W Arrowsmith, Bristol